FROM FARM TO YOU

Pasta and Noodles

Carol Jones

CHELSEA HOUSE PUBLISHERS
A Haights Cross Communications Company

Philadelphia

HERRICK DISTRICT LIBRARY
300 S. River Avenue
Holland, MI 49423

JUN 1 3 2003

This edition first published in 2003 in the United States of America by Chelsea House Publishers, a subsidiary of Haights Cross Communications.

All rights reserved. No part of this publication may be reproduced or transmitted in any form or by any means without the written permission of the publisher.

Chelsea House Publishers
1974 Sproul Road, Suite 400
Broomall, PA 19008-0914

The Chelsea House world wide web address is www.chelseahouse.com

Library of Congress Cataloging-in-Publication Data Applied for.
ISBN 0-7910-7004-2

First published in 2002 by
MACMILLAN EDUCATION AUSTRALIA PTY LTD
627 Chapel Street, South Yarra, Australia, 3141

Copyright © Carol Jones 2002
Copyright in photographs © individual photographers as credited

Edited by Anne McKenna
Text design by Judith Summerfeldt Grace
Cover design by Judith Summerfeldt Grace
Illustration on p. 19 by Pat Kermode, Purple Rabbit Productions

Printed in China

Acknowledgements
The author wishes to thank Maria, Andrew and Tony Reitano and Carmela Cambria of Pasta Fresca for their help with the writing of this book.

Cover photographs: Bowl of noodles courtesy of Imageaddict, pasta shells courtesy of Getty Images/Photodisc.

APL/Corbis © Julia Waterlow, p. 4, © Carl and Anne Purcell, pp. 8–9 (main), © W. Wayne Lockwood, M.D., p. 19, © Vittoriano Rastelli, p. 23; The Art Archive/Museo della Civilita Romana Rome/Dagli Orti, p. 5; Copper Leife/Craig Forsythe, pp. 8 (bottom), 20–1, [20 and 21 courtesy of Goodman Fielder], 22, 24–6 (bottom), [22, 24, and 25 (top) courtesy of Orgran Foods, 26 courtesy of Safeway], 28 (Lebanon); Getty Images/Photodisc, pp. 9 (bottom), 16–17, 28–9 (map), 28 (Thailand), Image Bank, p. 18, Eyewire, 29 (Japan); Imageaddict, pp. 28 (Italy and China), 29 (Australia); Carol Jones, pp. 3 (top and bottom right), 10–15; Mary Evans Picture Library, pp. 6–7; National Pasta Association, pp. 3 (top and bottom left), 28 (Malaysia), 29 (USA); Courtesy of Orgran Foods, p. 27 (top).

While every care has been taken to trace and acknowledge copyright, the publisher tenders their apologies for any accidental infringement where copyright has proved untraceable.

Contents

The world of pasta and noodles　4

The history of pasta and noodles　5

Kinds of pasta and noodles　8

How pasta is made　10

The pasta factory　16

Pasta and noodles around the world　28

Make your own pappardelle pasta　30

Glossary　31

Index　32

The world of pasta and noodles

Noodles, pasta, mein or pho are shaped pieces of cooked dough eaten in different countries of the world.

Noodles and pasta are an important part of Asian, Italian and other culture's diets. **Immigrants** from these areas have taken noodles to other parts of the world, and now people in countries such as Australia, Canada and the United States also enjoy eating noodles.

Noodles can be made from wheat, rice, barley, buckwheat or even mung bean flour. They can be fresh or dried, long or short, plain or filled. In some parts of the world they are even eaten as dessert.

Noodles are an important part of the Chinese diet.

The history of pasta and noodles

Noodles and pasta have a long and tangled history going back at least 2,000 years.

Many countries claim to have invented noodles: China, Japan, Korea, and of course Italy. We cannot be sure exactly where noodles first came from. They may have been invented in several places at different times. But we do know that the Chinese were eating noodles made from wheat flour 2,000 years ago, and so were the people of Ancient Rome.

In Roman times, people were cooking a dish with thin strips of noodle which they called lagana. Poor people ate it cooked in a broth. Rich people ate it served in layers with meat and sauce — just like today's lasagne.

Ancient Romans harvesting wheat

Firsts

A kind of lasagne was first served in Roman times. It is mentioned in a 2,000-year-old cookbook by the writer Apicio.

Noodles also have a long history in Japan. One story says that the Koreans brought soba noodles made from buckwheat to Japan in the 1100s. Another story says that Japanese udon noodles made from wheat flour are based on a Chinese recipe brought to Japan as early as the 800s.

A thousand years ago, Arab travelers from the **Middle East** carried a kind of dried noodle with them to eat as they traveled by ship or camel caravan through countries around the Mediterranean Sea.

Arab people traveling in camel caravans carried a kind of dried noodle to eat on their journeys.

Strange but true!

Udon noodles were so important in Kagawa on the Japanese island of Shikoku that new brides were expected to include noodle-making equipment as part of their **dowry**. Today there are nearly 3,000 noodle shops in Kagawa.

Noodle-like foods were known throughout Europe and the Middle East during the **Middle Ages**. Some were boiled, then fried or grilled. Others were stuffed like ravioli. By 1500, pasta was becoming a dish often eaten by the richer people of Italy. It was fresh and made by hand. By about 1700, hand-powered machines were invented to cut and press the pasta. It could then be dried in the sun.

The invention of electricity production in the late 1800s allowed pasta to be made by large machines in huge batches.

Strings of pasta hanging out to dry in Italy in the 1800s

Famous noodle tales

In the 1200s, the famous Italian traveller Marco Polo brought some noodles from China back to Italy. There is a story that the Italians first got their pasta from that sample. In fact they had already been making it for more than 1,000 years.
Thomas Jefferson brought a macaroni-making machine to the United States in 1789 after serving as Ambassador to France. He later became President of the United States.

Kinds of pasta and noodles

There are three main kinds of noodles or pasta: fresh, dried and pre-cooked. The flour for these noodles can be made from wheat, rice, corn, mung bean and other products. Noodles are long and thin, while pasta comes in almost endless shapes and sizes.

A Chinese noodle maker pulls and stretches dough into noodles.

1. Fresh pasta and noodles

Fresh noodles and pasta are made from the same ingredients as dried ones, but they are usually eaten within a few days of being made. Most fresh noodles and pasta are made from wheat flour or rice flour. They come in many shapes and sizes. In Italy they are sometimes stuffed with a filling such as meat or cheese. Some Chinese restaurants still employ noodle makers, who pull fresh dough into noodles with their hands while diners watch.

Pre-cooked noodles are quick to prepare.

8

2. Dried pasta and noodles

Dried pasta and noodles are dried in machines with hot moist air. Once dried and packaged, they can last for months or even years. In Italy, dried pasta made from wheat flour is most popular. Noodles made from rice flour, such as Vietnamese pho, are popular in southern China and Southeast Asia, where not much wheat is grown. Dried noodles take longer to cook than fresh noodles. They are sold in bundles, blocks or loose in packs.

3. Pre-cooked pasta and noodles

Noodles are often sold pre-cooked and this makes them quick and easy to prepare. Children love canned spaghetti and pasta shapes. Pasta shapes are often used in dried and canned soups. Instant noodles, to which you just add water and flavoring, are eaten in many parts of the world.

Dried pasta

Preservation

In the Middle Ages, Arabs living on the island of Sicily (now part of Italy) began drying pasta. Dried pasta could be stored for long sea voyages. Many ships sailed back and forth between this island and Italian cities, and soon the dried pasta of Sicily became known throughout the region.

How pasta is made

Dried pasta and noodles are usually made in large factories. However, there are many small local stores that make fresh pasta and noodles.

The pasta makers shown here are making pasta in a small factory to sell in their shop. They produce fresh pasta in many shapes, sizes and flavors. Fresh pasta is lighter and silkier than dried pasta.

Raw vegetables such as spinach or pumpkin may be added to make colored pastas. Dried potato is used for the cooked pasta-like dumplings called gnocchi.

Ingredients

The following ingredients are used to make the pasta:
- **semolina** — a coarse flour made from a hard wheat called durum wheat
- eggs — very fresh and at room temperature
- salt
- water
- spinach — for making green pasta.

Large containers and measuring scoops are used in pasta making.

A cutting machine like this can be set to different sizes and shapes by changing the metal die.

A metal die used for making short pasta

Tools and equipment

In the past, home cooks made the dough on a counter and cut it with a knife. Now, they usually use a food processor to mix the dough and a small hand-turned pasta machine to cut it.

Pasta makers use similar tools to those used at home, only much bigger. The tools used to make this pasta are:

- large containers and measuring scoops
- a dough-mixing machine
- large pasta-cutting machines with metal **dies**
- wooden trays.

The pasta maker measures the flour.

11

Method

Mixing the dough

The pasta maker measures out the correct quantities of flour, egg, water and salt. If a colored pasta is being made, raw vegetables such as spinach or tomato are also added. The ingredients are then tipped into the dough-mixing machine.

Inside the machine, metal blades **rotate**, stirring the ingredients. At first the mixture is dry and crumbly. The pasta makers can see when the dough is ready. It needs to be a little sticky, not too moist or too dry and crumbly. This takes 15 to 30 minutes.

Flour is placed in the top of the mixing machine. Dough is pressed out at the bottom.

Pressing the dough

A plastic **cylinder** is placed at the bottom of the mixing machine. The dough is pressed out of the machine between metal rollers, forming a sheet of dough.

The sheet rolls around the plastic cylinder. This cylinder can be placed into one of the other pressing and cutting machines.

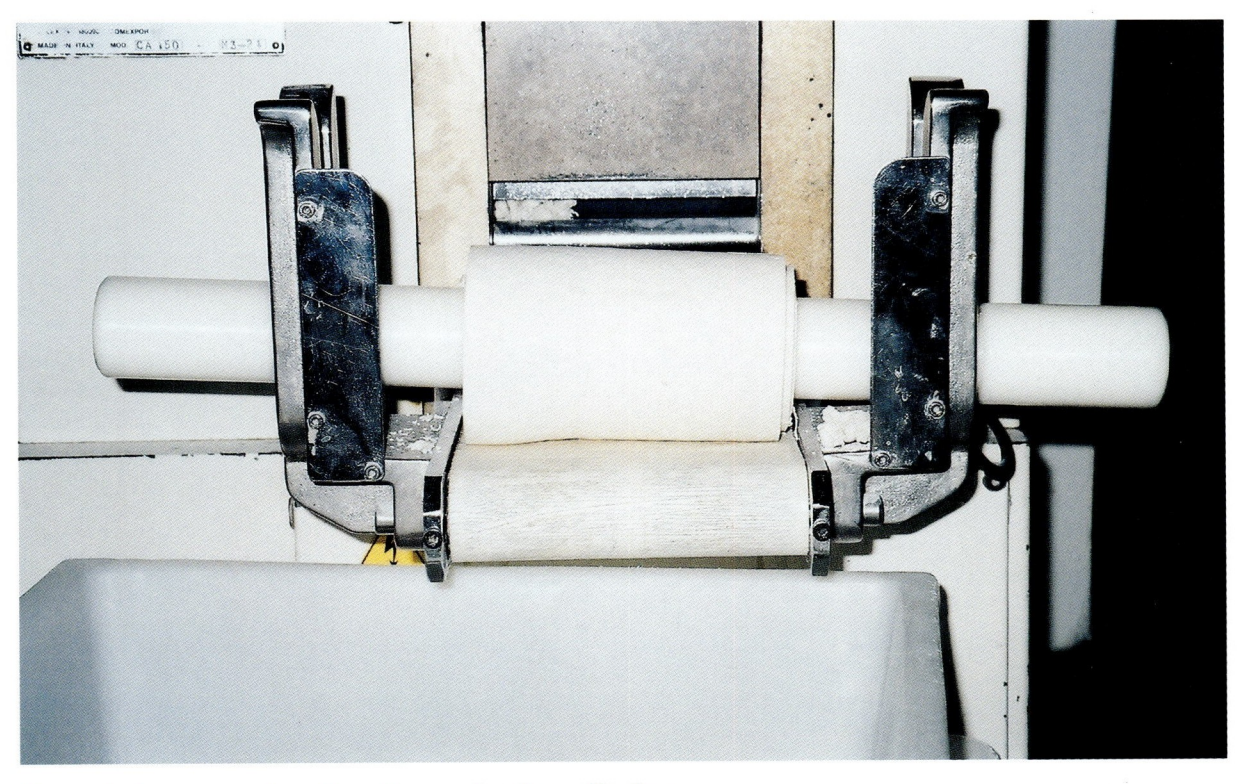

Dough is pressed out onto a plastic cylinder.

Cutting the pasta

The pasta cutter can be set to different thicknesses, lengths and widths. It is used for making fettuccine or other flat and long pastas. The plastic cylinder of pressed dough is placed on top of the cutting machine. It feeds the sheet of dough into the cutting machine. Inside the machine, metal cylinders with sharp grooves like blades rotate. As they rotate, the dough is cut and comes out of the machine in strips. The pasta makers carefully gather the long strips of pasta and fold them gently onto a wooden tray.

A different cutting machine is used to make short or hollow pastas. To make macaroni or penne, dough is pushed through a metal die with holes cut in it. Small pieces of dough come out of the machine shaped like little tubes.

The dough is fed into the cutting machine to be cut to shape.

Short pastas are pushed through a metal die.

Selling the pasta

The finished pasta is stacked onto plastic trays and refrigerated for sale in the shop. It can be kept here for up to four days. The shop sells many different kinds of long pasta, including skinny spaghetti, wide fettuccine and tagliatelle, and the strange, crinkly shaped mafalda.

The pasta makers also make hollow pastas such as macaroni, and filled pastas such as cannelloni and ravioli. Many small pasta makers also cook their own sauces, such as tomato sauce made with onion and spinach.

Thin spaghetti comes out of the cutting machine.

This pasta maker also makes sauces to eat with the fresh pasta.

The shop's refrigerator displays many kinds of pasta.

15

The pasta factory

Most of the dried pasta we buy is made in large factories. It is usually made from wheat flour.

From farm to consumer

Follow the flowchart to see how wheat is grown, **processed**, made into pasta in large factories and transported to stores for sale to the **consumer**.

Read more about each stage of the pasta-making process and how pasta is marketed and sold on pages 18 to 27. Look for the flowchart symbols that represent each stage of the process.

Farming the wheat
Farmers grow wheat on fairly flat land that is not too wet or too dry. When the wheat is ripe, it is **harvested**.

Packaging the pasta
Packaging materials may be made elsewhere and delivered to the **manufacturer**.
Pasta is packaged at the factory in bags or boxes.

Transport and storage
Packaged pasta is loaded onto **pallets** and transported to stores or sent to large consumers such as other food manufacturers.

Transport and storage
Harvested wheat is taken from the farm by truck to silos for storage. It is later taken to a flour mill.

Processing the wheat
At the flour mill, the wheat is ground into flour for making pasta.

Manufacturing the pasta
In large pasta factories, the flour is mixed with other ingredients to form dough that is made into pasta ready for packaging.

Transport and storage
Flour is taken in large tanker trucks from the flour mill to the pasta factory.

Marketing and selling pasta
Stores can keep dried pasta on shelves for a long time but fresh pasta must be sold quickly to consumers.

Buying the pasta
The consumer buys pasta from the store. Dried pasta may be stored for more than a year. Fresh pasta must be refrigerated and eaten soon.

Farming the wheat

Wheat is grown on fairly flat land that is not too wet or too dry. Wheat farmers use machines for **sowing** and harvesting their crops.

Wheat can be planted at different times of the year. Farmers who live in mild climates grow winter wheat. They plant winter wheat in fall and harvest it in spring or summer. Farmers in cooler climates grow spring wheat. They plant spring wheat in spring and harvest it in summer. Spring wheat matures faster, but winter wheat produces more kernels.

Huge wheat crops are grown in the United States, Canada, India, Russia and France.

Farm workers
Farmers and farm hands
Truck drivers
Workers at the grain elevator
Railway workers

Transport and storage

After harvesting, the wheat grains are taken by truck to a grain elevator. Trucks empty the wheat into large pits, then a conveyor belt carries the grain to the top of a large storage bin.

Farm machinery

Modern wheat farmers use many machines. A plow or cultivator prepares the soil for planting. A drill combines seed and **fertilizer** and drops them into **furrows**. These machines are pulled by tractors. Many farmers also use a boomspray to spray chemicals for weed and pest control. When the grain is ripe, a combine cuts the heads of the wheat and separates the grain from the **chaff**.

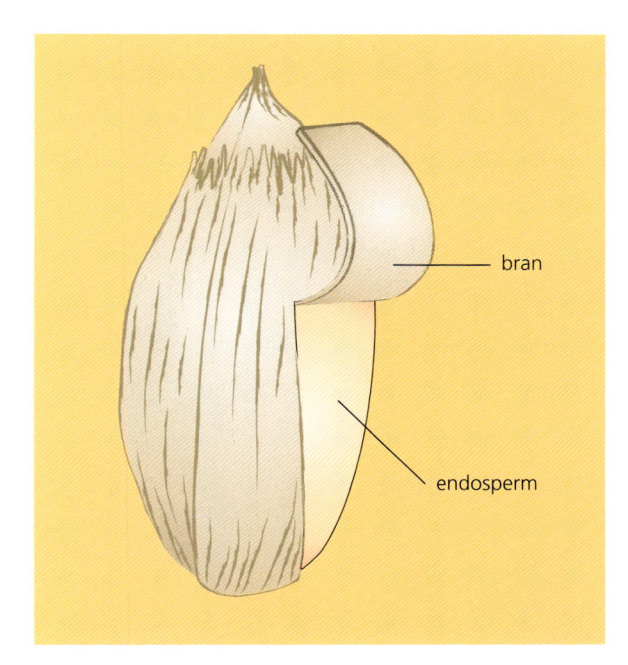

A grain of wheat

Harvesting the wheat

Conservation

Wheat takes **nutrients** from the soil. To replace these, some farmers rotate crops every year. After a field has grown wheat, the farmer might plant another crop such as corn or soybeans to put nutrients back into the soil, or leave the field unplanted for the season.

The wheat must be kept dry and free of insects. From the grain elevator, wheat is loaded into railroad cars and transported to a large grain terminal for shipping. There, different types of wheat may be blended for flour mills, or the grain may be inspected for shipping overseas.

19

Processing the wheat

At the flour mill, wheat for making pasta or noodles is processed. It is graded, cleaned, blended, soaked, ground, sifted and ground again to make flour.

First, wheat is inspected and graded for quality before it is sorted into groups. Different wheats are used for different products. Pasta and noodles are usually made from a hard wheat such as durum wheat.

Grain is cleaned to remove any stones, dust and weed seeds. It is soaked in water for 10 to 20 hours. This toughens the outer **bran** layer to make it easier to separate, and softens the inner **endosperm**. Whole-wheat flour is made from both parts of the wheat kernel, but white flour is made using only the endosperm.

These machines sift the wheat.

Transport and storage

Flour is stored in bags or bulk bins for three days. Then it is blown through a chute into a waiting truck. Trucks are sealed so that dust cannot get into the flour.

Sieving and crushing the wheat

The wheat is fed into grooved roller mills that rotate toward each other. The bran is broken away from the endosperm, which is crushed to make semolina. This is sieved and separated into bran and semolina by air blown through machines called plansifters. The semolina is crushed further in smooth roller mills and sifted again. Semolina will be crushed many times until it is the right texture. Flour for pasta making may be quite coarse.

Wheat is crushed in roller mills.

Flour is blown into trucks through a sealed chute.

Strange but true!

The grooves on old-fashioned stone mills were very important for breaking open the grain. After about 100 hours of milling, the grooves wore down and had to be repaired. It was the job of a traveling millwright to chip away at the stones. This could take 18 hours.

Trucks are weighed to measure the weight of the flour, which is then delivered to pasta factories.

Mill workers
Production-line workers
Engineers
Food scientists
Food technologists
Transport workers

Manufacturing the pasta

Large pasta factories are fully **automated**. Enormous machines controlled by computers handle every part of the pasta-making process.

Machines called dosers measure the exact quantities of raw ingredients and feed them into the mixer. Wet ingredients, such as egg and water, are combined with dry ingredients, such as flour and dried vegetable powders, in the dough-mixing machine. This machine is like a large enclosed tub.

After mixing, the dough is **kneaded**. Most kneading machines in large pasta factories work in a **vacuum** so that the dough stays a yellow color. If oxygen gets into the dough it will turn gray.

Mixing the dough

Transport and storage

After the flour arrives from the flour mill, it is stored in a grain elevator.

Shaping the dough

After kneading, the dough is pushed through a cylinder inside which a screw rotates. This screw pushes the dough toward the press where a die is set. The pressure from the pushing screw forces the dough through the openings in the die. The pasta shapes are pushed out in the shape of the die. For example, they may be round and hollow, or shell-shaped. Special machines like hoists are used to change the heavy dies for making different-shaped pastas in large factories.

This machine cuts the spaghetti.

Pasta moves through the plant mechanically. For example, long pasta is moved on carrying sticks. Short pasta is moved on a **conveyor belt**.

Additives

Apart from ingredients for flavor and taste, such as egg, spinach, tomato or pumpkin, most dried pastas do not contain **artificial** colorings, flavors or **preservatives**.

Drying the pasta

Long pasta comes out of the die like a curtain. A machine called a spreader cuts the pasta to the right length and places it on a metal stick, which will carry the pasta along the production line. The carrying stick keeps the pasta straight and stops it from sticking together.

The curtain of pasta is then sent through a series of large driers. Hot moist air blows around the pasta to dry it. Then it is cooled with cool moist air.

Pasta is dried on racks and in a heat-sensitive machine.

Factory workers

Production-line workers

Engineers

Food scientists

Food technologists

Packaging the pasta

Pasta may be packaged and transported to stores or sent directly to large consumers such as restaurants.

Before packaging, the pasta is checked for quality. A sample may be tested by cooking it. Machines weigh and pack the finished pasta in bags or boxes. Sometimes, fragile pasta shapes such as lasagne are packed by hand so that they do not break.

Packaged pasta is packed into cartons and loaded onto pallets for transport to supermarkets and smaller stores. Some pasta is packaged in bulk and delivered to other food manufacturers for use in soups, canned goods and pre-prepared meals.

Pasta is weighed and packed by machine.

Packaging workers
Production-line workers
Graphic designers
Forklift drivers
Transport workers

Transport and storage

Pallets are loaded onto large trucks with forklifts. Some loads are taken to ports for shipping overseas in containers. Other loads are delivered to stores and food manufacturers.

25

Marketing and selling pasta

Dried pasta and noodles stay fresh for a long time, but fresh noodles and pasta must be sold quickly to the consumer.

Workers from pasta and noodle companies, called merchandisers, visit stores to find out what kind and how much of each product the store needs. Some supermarkets sell many different kinds of pasta and noodles. Companies might also arrange tastings in stores to advertise new products to consumers.

Large noodle and pasta companies can also afford to advertise their products to a larger audience. They might place ads in magazines or on television. Some companies have their own websites to tell consumers about their products.

Marketing and sales workers
Shop owners and supermarket managers
Merchandisers
Shelf-fillers
Checkout operators
Graphic designers
Copywriters

Supermarkets sell all kinds of pasta and noodles.

Buying pasta

Consumers can buy dried pasta and noodles from the supermarket or store shelves. In the past, most of the noodles and pasta sold in supermarkets were dried or pre-cooked. To buy fresh pasta and noodles, consumers needed to visit a special fresh pasta store or an Asian food store where the noodles were made in the store or delivered fresh daily. They would be kept refrigerated for only a few days before sale.

Now, with improved packaging, supermarkets sell fresh pasta and noodles in their refrigerated display cases. Pasta and noodles can be vacuum-packed in plastic to keep them fresher for longer, or sealed in specially designed plastic packs for up to a few weeks.

Consumers can choose from many varieties of pasta and noodles. There are many ways to cook pasta and noodles at home — tossed with sauce, baked, stir-fried or simmered in soup.

This pasta company provides recipes for consumers.

Consumers can buy noodles that are cooked by adding boiling water.

Home storage

Dried pasta and noodles can be stored at home for up to a year in a cool, dry place. Fresh noodles or pasta bought loose should be refrigerated. They are best cooked and eaten soon after you bring them home. Check the use-by date on packaged fresh noodles and pasta.

27

Pasta and noodles around the world

Italy is the home of hundreds of different kinds of pasta. They can be boiled, baked or used in soup. Some of the most well known noodles are spaghetti, tagliatelle, fettuccine and pappardelle.

China has many kinds of fresh and dried wheat noodles called mian in Mandarin and mein in Cantonese. Other popular noodles are dried rice-stick noodles and mung-bean or cellophane noodles. Noodles are usually fried or served in soup.

In Middle Eastern countries such as Lebanon, fine thread-like vermicelli noodles are often used to create sweet cakes such as knaffeh.

Malaysia has its own version of wheat and rice noodles. They can be served fried or in soup.

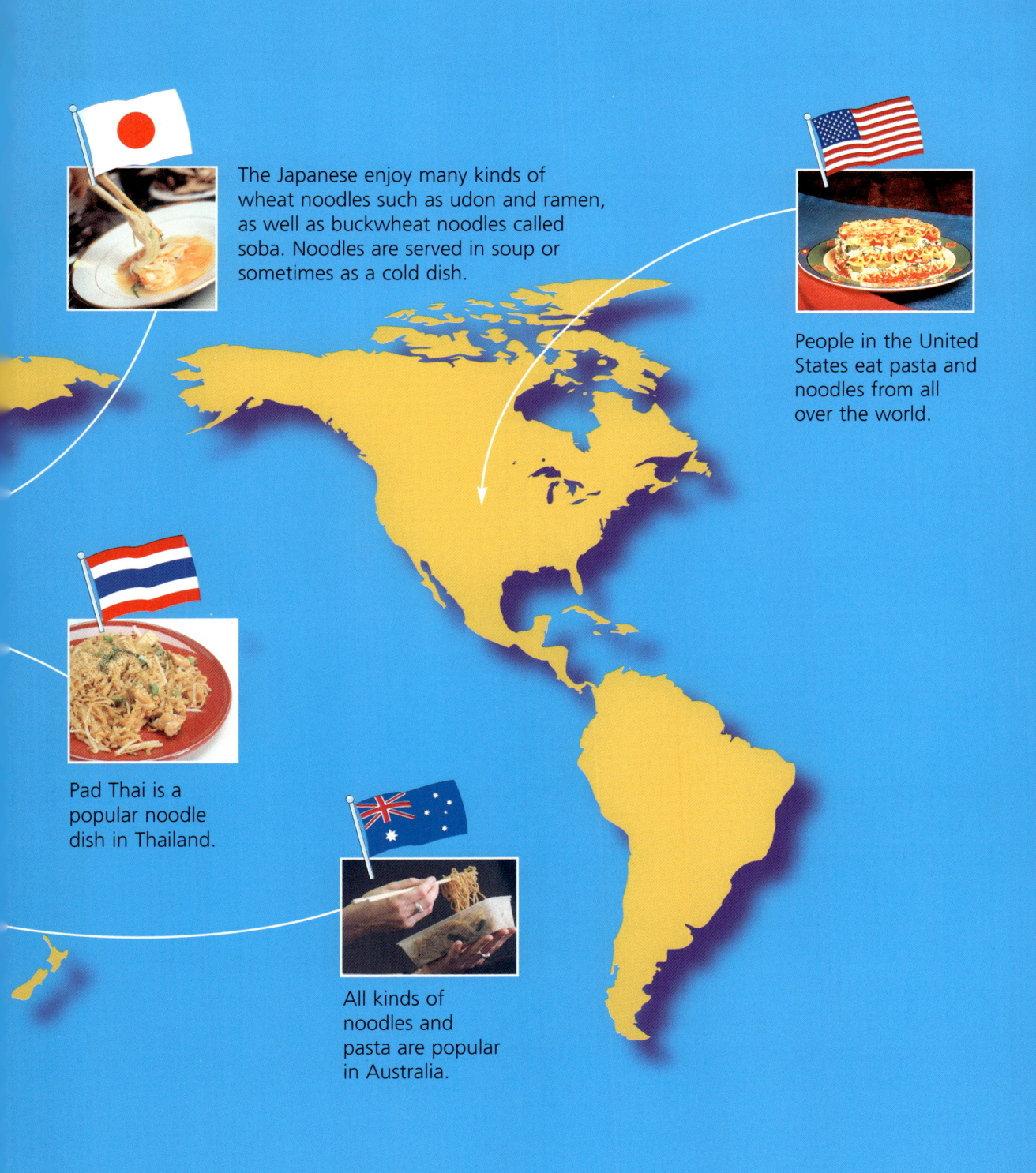

The Japanese enjoy many kinds of wheat noodles such as udon and ramen, as well as buckwheat noodles called soba. Noodles are served in soup or sometimes as a cold dish.

People in the United States eat pasta and noodles from all over the world.

Pad Thai is a popular noodle dish in Thailand.

All kinds of noodles and pasta are popular in Australia.

29

Make your own pappardelle pasta

Use this recipe to make a wide, ribbon pasta called pappardelle at home with help from an adult.

Pappardelle

Ingredients
- $2\frac{1}{3}$ cups of flour
- 1 teaspoon of salt
- 3 eggs, lightly beaten
- extra flour

Equipment
- bowl
- wooden spoon
- clean counter
- plastic wrap
- knife
- rolling pin
- tea towel
- large pot
- colander
- large pan

Method
1. Place the flour and salt in a bowl. Make a well in the flour and slowly add the eggs with a wooden spoon. Then dip your fingers in some extra flour and work the flour and eggs together until they form a dough.
2. Tip the dough onto a floured counter. Fold it in half and gently press down (knead). Keep kneading for at least 5 minutes. Then wrap the ball of dough in plastic wrap and let it rest for 30 minutes.
3. Place the dough on the floured counter and cut it in half. Re-wrap one half.
4. Flatten the dough with the heel of your hand to make a rough circle. Use a floured rolling pin to roll the dough to $\frac{1}{8}$ inch thick. Sprinkle with flour to stop it from sticking. You may need to sprinkle flour more than once.
5. Cut into long strips about $\frac{3}{4}$ inch wide. Spread the strips on the floured tea towel for 15 minutes to dry. Follow steps 4 and 5 for the remaining dough.
6. Ask an adult to heat a big pan of boiling water and a little salt until it boils. Then tip in the pasta. Stir to stop the pasta sticking. Cook for 2 to 3 minutes until still a little chewy.
7. Drain in a colander and serve with your favorite sauce.

Glossary

artificial — made by people

automated — a machine that works with little human help

bran — the tough outer layer of the wheat grain

chaff — bits of straw left after wheat heads are separated from stalk

consumer — person who buys goods or services

conveyor belt — an endless strip of material, such as rubber, on rollers used to move something

cylinder — a shape like a barrel

dies — blocks of metal used to shape things

dowry — property brought by a woman to her husband at marriage

endosperm — the white inner part of the wheat from which flour is made

fertilizer — a substance added to soil to help plants grow

food technologists — workers who scientifically test or treat food

furrows — shallow trenches

harvested — picked the crop

immigrants — people who come from another country

kneaded — worked and pressed the dough

manufacturer — person or company that makes goods

Middle Ages — period in Europe from 500 A.D. to 1500 A.D.

Middle East — area around eastern Mediterranean Sea, from Turkey to North Africa

nutrients — food substances that help us stay healthy

pallets — large trays

preservatives — ingredients to keep food fresh

processed — treated in a special way

rotate — turn around

semolina — a coarse flour

sowing — planting

vacuum — absence of any gas

Index

A
advertising   26
Asia   4, 9
Australia   4, 29

B
bran   20–21
buckwheat   4, 29

C
Canada   4
China   5–9, 28
conservation   19
consumers   16–17, 26–27
cultivation   19
cutting pasta   13–14, 24

D
dried pasta   8–10, 16–17, 27

E
endosperm   20–21

F
farming   16, 18–19
fresh pasta   8, 10–15, 17, 27

H
harvesting   17, 18–19

I
Italy   4–5, 8–9, 28

J
Japan   5–6, 29

K
Korea   5–6

L
Lebanon   28

M
machines   7, 11–14, 18–19, 21–25
Malaysia   28
manufacturing   17, 22–24
marketing   17, 26
Middle East   6–7, 28
milling   21
mills   20, 22
mixing   11–12, 22
mung bean   4, 29

P
packaging   16, 25, 27
pre-cooked pasta   8–9, 27
preserving   9, 23
processing   17, 20–21

R
Rome   5

S
selling   17, 26–27
silos   18, 22
storage   16–25, 27
supermarkets   25–27

T
Thailand   28
transport   16–25

U
United States   4, 7, 29

V
Vietnam   9

W
wheat   4, 16–18, 20
wheat flour   5–6, 8–9, 17, 20

WITHDRAWN FROM
HERRICK DISTRICT LIBRARY